Faerie Houses 11

Coloring Book

Stephany Elsworth

Copyright © 2019 by Stephany Elsworth
All rights reserved. No part of this publication may be reproduced, distributed, or transmitted in any form or by any means, including photocopying, recording, or other electronic or mechanical methods, without the prior written permission of the author.

Made in the USA
Monee, IL
22 September 2020